A COMPLETE

180°

*Stability, Flexibility and Mobility
in Business*

Anointed Press
PUBLISHERS

CHELTENHAM, MARYLAND
www.anointedpresspublishers.com

A COMPLETE

180°

Stability, Flexibility and Mobility in Business

Dr. Jason Henderson, DPT, MBA

A Complete 180°: Stability, Flexibility, and Mobility in Business

To Purchase Additional Books:

jhenderson@ergo180.com
www.OptimisticDiversity.com
www.amazon.com
Also available on Kindle
www.anointedpressgraphics.com

For Bulk Orders over 25 books, call
Anointed Press Publishers, (301) 782-2285

INGRAM DISTRIBUTION

Cover Design:

Anointed Press Graphics, Inc.
www.anointedpressgraphics.com
Copyright © 2018

Published by:

Anointed Press Publishers
(a subsidiary of Anointed Press Graphics, Inc.)
11191 Crain Highway
Cheltenham, MD 20623
(301) 782-2285

In collaboration with

Quantitative Quality Solution Systems

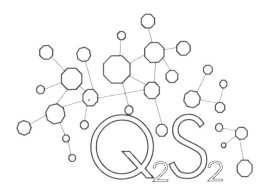

CONTENTS

LIST OF TABLES

AN EINTRODUCTION

I was 17 years old. A Senior at Central High School[i], in Philadelphia, PA. Sitting there, took my 'No. 2' pencil and chose – filled in – the circle beside my new focus at my new school; Florida Agricultural and Mechanical University[ii]. I passed over business, then pharmacy, hesitated at architecture, to finally take fate and I began my journey in to the next phase of growth in my life; training to be a physical therapist.

Understand, I had the aptitude to fulfill any of those considered, but at that young age, I chose physical therapy and have grown from a student to a therapist, to now a service provider and doctor of the science. Now I share my knowledge and welcome opportunities to speak on business development, leadership, community commitment, excellence at care and wisdom gathered in my experience.

My name is Jason S. Henderson, DPT, MBA; I am business owner and as responsibility leads ownership, I insured my business by completing an MBA in 2013, releasing major gains into my business.

BOOK CONCEPT

In this book find many tools implemented within my organizations. This book is for those businesses unable to take advantage of their market, experiencing limited movement, slow regeneration and restricted potential. To make best used of this collection, be attentive to special 180° eWords they are keys to Full Motion in Business.

To begin, any group should assess processes by defining or creating them. Do so in a way that identities or indicates metrics; think about how data points are gathered and group them as quantitative[iii], qualitative [iv], or both. Note: Organization is essential - If an organization has parts or processes that are undefined, it should take time to define those areas. If not, whatever growth, gains or losses out of that part or process of the organization, will not be understood. Organization is a requirement for business.

This book makes 18 scored measurements: Collect scores and evaluate business stability, flexibility and mobility. Providing scale and scope to improve business practices and secure productivity well into the future by answering each assessment, honestly.

DEDICATED

Almost 20 years ago I chose again, only this time it was to join a group and begin what would become: Ergo Solutions, Ergo OccMed, and a nonprofit, Ergo Resolutions. Today I work for my company, every day, providing quality care in the Washington DC metropolitan statistical area.[v] I have served as CEO and CIO of Ergo Solutions for ten years and executive director of Ergo Resolutions for nearly eight years.

My experience is unique, extensive and diverse. This work was built to ensure those who pursue the practice of business excellence.

Congratulations on making a motion to business: Gain 180° of motion in all business and organizational efforts.

Dr. J. Henderson, DPT, MBA

STATIONARY ARM AS STABILITY

Purpose of Stability Training

Muscle stiffness is a term that is used to describe the spring-like quality of muscle. When a muscle has high stiffness, increased force is required to cause lengthening of that muscle or to perturb it. Muscle stiffness has been described in the biomechanical and neurophysiological literature as one of the most crucial variables in joint stabilization. In the knee, a link has been established between receptors in the ligaments of the joint and muscle stiffness.

Dynamic stabilization or the use of exercise to promote joint stabilization occurs when tonic (postural and slow twitch muscle) units are activated. These tonic motor units are activated during tonic continuous low load activation of muscle, maximizing muscle stiffness. What we are talking about here is asking the muscle to contract gently, not maximally, and to be able to sustain that contraction over a time. This can be influenced by the speed of the activity or exercise, as well as the type of muscle contraction you are trying to acquire. Muscle contractions that are performed in the shortened range of the muscle length are going to be critical in establishing the sensitivity and optimal functional capacity of the sensory feedback system in the muscle.

Businesses likewise must have stability. The optimal functional capacity of the business requires sensory feedback just like muscles do. An assessment of this section will encourage you to solicit subjective information from your clients, customers, patients, employees, managers, executives and stakeholders. Anywhere there is weakness, it is important to gain strength for stability. These six terms are used to describe the areas that must be strengthened to ensure Administration and Management Stability:

ngagement

ffectiveness

xecution

xpertise

xperience

thics

# NGAGEMENT

ENGAGEMENT: *Emotional involvement or commitment; to get and keep interest; to hire; to bind to something; to induce participation, to pledge oneself.*[vi]

"Relationships matter where value goes beyond pricing!" - *Susan Bailey, Hospital Administrator*

"The formula for sustainability" - *Olu Ezeani DPT, principal Ergo Solution and Ergo OccMed*

Early in my career, while a staff therapist in acute care, home health and hospital settings, I learned the importance of engagement. Much of my engaging behavior came from modeling after therapists that I admired. How I engaged with customers and staff and supervisors was important to keep me focused on the job. At Providence/ Carroll Manor Hospital, the rehab staff was trained on engagement by Jeffrey Wright PT, one of my mentors in the profession.

In the rehab environment cooperation with fellow co-workers is important. Some of my best friends in life are therapists that I worked with. Many may not know that there is a reward in cooperation. I read "reward structures are integral to driving cooperative behavior. These structures can be implemented by designing instructional activities more strategically, which encourages learners to pursue joint goals while still remaining individually accountable for their performance." As a staffer, I valued the experience of "cooperative learning, reward structures and peer coaching." As a staff PT, I want to be in a learning environment with a multi-disciplinary approach with opportunity to exchange expertise, knowledge and information with other professionals. I like cooperative learning; it is as an excellent strategy for developing educational outcomes. I have observed over the past 20 years in the Physical Therapy profession that competitive learning is a great way to promote positive self-esteem and excellence in practice.

I have trained under great leadership by managers and directors that helped my professional growth even when adversity arose in my life. I had the pleasure of working in a profession where engagement was necessary to help us to understand more deeply the reward of cooperation.

I encourage students and staff PTs to develop positive interdependence and individual accountability. Positive interdependence means that group members must work together to gain recognition for their efforts. My engagement enabled me to grow and to move up to becoming recognized as a leader among my peers. This allowed my professional growth to progress to management and leadership. Along with the upward bound movement is the elevation of pay and that was my reward.

After my first 7 years as a staff PT I learned to master soft skills like engagement. As I became a manager I always taught that clinical facilities and professional staff must also recognize that achieving professional mastery takes many years of practice and can be hastened by involving others in one's professional development journey.

How important is engagement to a company or organization? In business, apply the definition towards customers and employees.

Realize "if customers are not satisfied, they will eventually find other suppliers to meet their needs. Poor performance from this perspective is thus a leading indicator of future decline, even though the current financial picture may look good." [vii]

KNOW WHO IS BOSS

Be in business to service customer needs and do that by knowing what customers want. Truly listen to customers; they inform what they want and how to provide good service. Never forget that the customer makes service provision and compensation possible.

BE A GOOD LISTENER

Take the time to identify customer needs by asking questions and concentrating on what the customer is really saying. Listen to their words, tone of voice, body language, and most importantly, how they feel. Beware of making assumptions— think intuitively. Try knowing what the customer wants by thinking of what you would want if you were in the customer's position. Try to know what three things are most important to your customer.

EFFECTIVE LISTENING AND UNDIVIDED ATTENTION

This is particularly important because there is a great danger of being distracted or preoccupied. Look around to see who else you could be selling to or paying attention to.

IDENTIFY AND ANTICIPATE NEEDS

Customers do not buy products or services; they buy good feelings and solutions to problems. For most customers, needs are emotional rather than logical. Communicate regularly to be aware of problems or upcoming needs.

MAKE CUSTOMERS FEEL IMPORTANT AND APPRECIATED

Treat them as individuals. Always use names and find ways to sincerely compliment. People value genuineness.

It creates good feelings and trust. Think about ways to generate good feelings about doing business with you. Customers are very sensitive and know whether a business really cares about them. Thank them at every opportunity.

BE SURE BODY LANGUAGE CONVEYS RELIABILITY

Words and actions should be congruent.

HELP CUSTOMERS UNDERSTAND SYSTEMS

An organization may have the 'world's best' systems for getting things done, but if customers don't understand them, customers can get confused, impatient and angry. Take time to explain how the system in your organization works and how the process is beneficial.

Make sure customers know and feel how important they are to your system processes and organization.

APPRECIATE THE POWER OF "YES"

Always look for ways to help your customers. When they have a request (as long as it is reasonable) say that it will be met. Plan the then execute the actions, later.

Look for ways to make doing business, simple. Always keep promises made to customers.

KNOW HOW TO APOLOGIZE

When something goes wrong, apologize. It is easy, and customers like it. The customer may not always be right, but the customer must always win. Deal with problems immediately and let customers know how the problem was solved. Make it simple for customers to complain. Value complaints by using them as opportunities to improve. Even if customers are having a bad day, go beyond the expected to make them feel comfortable.

GIVE MORE THAN EXPECTED

The future of all companies lies in keeping customers happy, think of ways to elevate above the competition. Consider these:

- What is offered that customers cannot gain elsewhere?
- What could be a way to follow up and thank people even when they do not buy?
- How you could provide customers with an experience they do not expect?

GET REGULAR FEEDBACK

Encourage and welcome suggestions about how to improve. There are several ways to find out what customers think and feel about service offerings.

- Listen carefully to what is said.
- Check back regularly to see how things are going.

• Provide a method that invites constructive criticism, comments and suggestions.

TREAT EMPLOYEES WELL

Employees are your internal customers and need a regular dose of appreciation. Thank them and find ways to let them know how important they are. Treat your employees with respect and chances are they will have a higher regard for customers. Appreciation starts from the top. Treating employees well is equally important to treating customers well.

WORKING IN A CULTURALLY UNFAMILIAR ENVIRONMENT:

To have a successful business culture, it is important that managers maintain a high level of employee engagement. To gain insight into levels of engagement within a new organization, implement the Utrecht Work Engagement Scale (UWES). This scale allows organizations to measure levels of work engagement. "The UWES covers three dimensions: vigor, dedication and absorption. They are conceptually regarded as the opposite of burnout and are scored on a 7pt frequency-rating scale, varying from 0 ('never') to 6 ('every day')." The questionnaire is made up of 17 questions and includes statements like 'I am bursting with energy every day in my work', 'time flies when I am at work' and 'my job inspires me.'

As Colquitt and company point out, high levels of engagement are linked to job satisfaction. As employees experience more satisfaction, employee performance goes up. Similarly, high levels of job satisfaction can lead to marked increases in organizational commitment.

TABLE 1 -
ENGAGEMENT EVALUATION TOOL

Complete table and totals to collect assessment.
Check the box of the "Yes" Column if the evaluation point applies to your organization;
Check the box of the "No" in the box if the evaluation point does not apply to your
organization. Each "Yes" answer is worth .83 points, record the value in the - Point
Value column.
Add points in the Point Value column.

ENGAGEMENT EVALUATION POINT	YES (.833 pts for each answer)	NO (0 pts for each answer)	POINT VALUE
Know who is boss?			
Identify and anticipate needs?			
Help customers understand your systems?			
Give more than expected?			
Be a good listener?			
Make customers feel important and appreciated: Relationship?			
Appreciate the power of "Yes"?			
Get regular feedback?			
Effective listening and undivided attention?			
Convey sincerity?			
Know how to apologize?			
Treat employees well: Internal Customer Appreciation?			
TOTAL – Note 8.3 points x 12 answers = 100			

EFFECTIVENESS

EFFECTIVENESS: *Producing a desired result; having an intended effect; corporate effectiveness is important to producing a desired effect[viii] - for example obtaining outcome goals.*

"Ergo Solutions is the national leader for inpatient rehabilitation hospitals in terms of revenue, number of hospitals, and patients treated and discharged. Achieving such status required analysis of corporate effectiveness."
- Jason Henderson, DPT, MBA and CEO of Ergo Solutions

Over time, I became a senior supervisor, working at Greater Southeast Community Hospital in Washington, D.C. I supervised the Outpatient department with seven therapists. I reported monthly and monitored visits versus no shows. I also carried a caseload of 20 patients, daily. I learned the importance of being effective as a clinical manager to meet the expectations of the director of rehab services. As a senior supervisor, I learned behaviors and actions that provided the conditions for improved learning, processes, thereby cultivating competitive advantages in the workplace and ultimately enhancing the viability of the organization. (Brueller and Carmeli)

I learned as a manager to build positive attributes. This made me effective with my staff – they were sure that they could depend on my leadership. Creating connections achieved in the 'office' must be bound by the parameters of "psychological safety and learning processes in the workplace" – these spaces create and stress the importance of "facilitating learning." To drive performance along with teaching and training in positive associations of team work, leaders must keep high standards and provide the pathway to achieve them. Excellence is possible at work. Create policies and processes that produce the desired results and make them repeatable. Write them down, test them, validate them and practice them.

How important is Effectiveness to a company or organization? A project management plan is the application of team knowledge, skills, tools and techniques to implement activities that meet project requirements.

Project management plans include:
- Scope
- Work Breakdown Structure
- Critical Pathway

- Operational effectiveness - The result of maximized output of invested resources. Effectiveness is measured and graded for quality, production and importance. There are positive impacts of operational effectiveness. Effectiveness is the direct result of efficiency.
- Operations strategy - The way a business is set up determines how effective it will be. The means of use of input and managing and producing an effective output is by way of the strategy developed by management.
- Operations sustainability - Sustainability enables a company or business to continue to thrive in production, revenue and importance.

TABLE 2 - EFFECTIVENESS EVALUATION TOOL

Complete table and totals to collect assessment.
Check the box of the "Yes" Column if the evaluation point applies to your organization; Check the box of the "No" in the box if the evaluation point does not apply to your organization. Each "Yes" answer is worth 1.0 points, record the value in the - Point Value column. Add points in the Point Value column.

EFFECTIVENESS-SIX SIGMA EVALUATION POINTS	YES (1.0 pts for each answer)	NO (0 pts for each answer)	POINT VALUE
Genuine focus on the customer?			
The 'Voice of the Customer' is the foundation to methodology data- and fact-driven management?			
Use data to prove that solutions work, and gains are sustained process focus?			
Improving processes ensures competitive advantage – delivering real value to customers Proactive management?			
Set/track goals, establish priorities, reward fire prevention?			
Collaboration without boundaries?			
Customer-centric; processes transcend departmental silos?			
Drive for perfection, tolerate failure?			
New ideas/approaches involve risk; overcome fear of mistakes?			
Bonus: Metrics developed?			
TOTAL – *Degree Potential x10*			

16

XECUTION

EXECUTION: *The mode or result of performance; the strategy.[ix]*

"Execution can be seen as luck (smiles). No, it's the critical drive with efficiency to meet expectation. It's doing what needs to be done and not being afraid to do it. It's the experience of the right people, doing the right thing at the right time." - *Sandy Douglass, Methodist Home, DCHCA Administrator of the year 2014*

How important is Execution to a company or organization? As a Director of rehab services at Grant Park HealthCare Center in Washington, DC, I managed the 297-bed skill and long-term nursing facility. I led a staff of 12 therapists to provide services in OT, PT, and SLP. I had to learn how to be an executive now as I was a part of the leadership of the home. I had deliverables and more expectations as I grew from a manager to now a director of rehab services. The skills required to manage and be an administrator were beyond what I learned in undergrad PT school. I had to develop more skills and abilities which included financial management, Informational management, networking, human resource management, daily operations, planning and strategy.

STRATEGY MAP: BALANCED SCORECARD

Similar to the way war strategies are developed, strategy maps show how to go about change for business. Strategy maps may be redesigned or reorganized as plans of action for execution (Norton, 2010).

Seek opportunities and measure them using a scorecard. Monitor and track business performance over time. The focus is integration of the scorecard as a process in policy, enhancing organization. This also exposes opportunities, and collects overall financial perspective, operations and human resource service data. Collecting data on changes and establishing metrics for finances, customer services, and internal processes as well as learning and growth processes, establishes objectives that allow focus on goal metrics. With such a tool, a company may proceed with confidence towards long term sustainability. Continued use yields maturity of processes defined within the scorecard.

At a 2008 conference of CEOs, Dr. David Norton listed the following issues and barriers that companies face the most.

They include the ability to:

- Execute.
- Execute consistently.
- React quickly and be flexible to the issue.

There is a need of a strategy and the need to execute.[x]

BALANCED SCORECARD (BSC)

The BSC attempts to measure and provide feedback for defining strategies and objectives. The future looks brighter by making changes and instituting metrics for finances, providing excellent customer services, refining internal processes and instituting a learning and growth process. Established objectives allow you to focus on measurable goals. Targets are easier to hit when visible. Meeting targets listed on the scorecard builds long-term sustainability as well as confidence. Your teams will gain maturity of processes described on the scorecard.

Core business must equal services.

- Deliver comprehensive, high-quality, cost-effective services.
- High skills and technology
- Provide progress, documentation, oversight of status, achievement of goals, planning, and functional outcomes.

- Provide a comprehensive interdisciplinary approach to service; this will lead to excellence and superior outcomes.

The strategy is to focus on these priorities: "The balanced scorecard retains traditional financial measures. Financial measures tell the story of past events, an adequate story for industrial age companies for which investments in long-term capabilities and customer relationships were not critical for success. These financial measures are inadequate, however, for guiding and evaluating the journey that information age companies must make to create future value through investment in customers, suppliers, employees, processes, technology, and innovation."[xi]

Implement BSC framework by applying five core principles:

- Translate strategy into operational terms.
- Align organization to the strategy.
- Make strategy everyone's job.
- Make strategy a continuous process.
- Mobilize change through executive leadership.[xii]

These metrics must be carefully designed, meaning these measures are not to be developed by outside consultants. Opposed to P&L[xiii], which shows the profit position of a company, BSC summarizes company assets, liabilities and shareholder equity at a point in time. "There is perhaps a need to include additional financial-related data, such as risk assessment and cost-benefit data, in this category."[xiv]

THE RATIO OF ACCOUNTS RECEIVABLES = VITALITY

The importance of revenue production is not greater than management and maintenance of the expenses for current ratio of liabilities: Maintain with minimal investors, focusing debt. Manage accounts receivables and payables, generalizing accounts receivable turnover ratio.

OBSERVE:

Receivables Turnover (rT) = *Net Credit Sales/Average accounts receivables*

Distributed over the year, receivables will convert 'rT' times.

It will take '365/ rT'days on average, to collect on receivables. A higher number of days indicates slow returns; a "cash-flow problem." Remember - ratios are only effective when used in comparison to other benchmarks, trends or industry standards. A turnover ratio well below the industry average would indicate much slower conversion of receivables than other companies. A much lower receivable to sales ratio, when compared, may indicate effective sales policies are in place to convert sales to cash on a quicker rate; study this trend data.

A 'Z-Score' is a statistical measurement of score relationship to the mean in a group of scores.[xv] Monitor market value on liability ratios, revenue to total asset ratios, working capital to total assets, EBIT to total assets and retained earnings to total asset ratios to keep a strong Z score over the fiscal year. To make sure of long term solvency, target scores above 3.0, comparatively, scores at and below 2.0 predict insolvency.

CORE COMPETENCIES

Those capabilities critical to a business achieving a competitive advantage are core competencies.

Starting points for analyzing core competencies include:

- Recognizing competition between businesses = a race for competence.
- Mastery of market position and market power.
- Focused attention on competencies for competitive advantage.

TABLE 3 - EXECUTION - BALANCED SCORECARD EVALUATION TOOL

Complete table and totals to collect assessment.
Check the box of the "Yes" Column if the evaluation point applies to your organization; Check the box of the "No" in the box if the evaluation point does not apply to your organization. Each "Yes" answer is worth 1.25 points, record the value in the - Point Value column. Add points in the Point Value column.

BALANCED SCORECARD AND CORE COMPETENCIES EVALUATION POINTS	YES (1.25 pts for each answer)	NO (0 pts for each answer)	POINT VALUE
Translate the strategy into operational terms?			
Align the organization to the strategy?			
Make strategy everyone's job?			
Make the strategy a continuous process?			
Mobilize change through executive leadership?			
Recognizing that competition between businesses is as much a race for competence?			
Mastery of market position and market power?			
The goal is to focus attention on competencies for competitive advantage?			
Bonus: Metrics developed?			
TOTAL – *Degree Potential x10*			

EXPERTISE

EXPERTISE: *The skills of an expert, having, involving or displaying special skills or knowledge derived from training or experience.*

"Strategic fit is an exercise for a company which believes it must adapt itself to the business environment. Strategic intent involves a more active process in which a company decides on its mission and goals and then actively seeks to carry out its plans. Gaining expertise is "an active, creative, hard-charging strategy." - *Sullivan*

As a business owner and clinical director of rehab services, at the Lisner-Louise-Dickson-Hurt Home and Jeanne Jugan Residence Home, I had to increase my level of expertise. My company was now hiring staff with powerful credentials. I had to invest in me even when I did not truly want to go back to school. As the company began to grow, I had to grow at the same pace or faster or it would leave me behind. I did not want to become extinct in the profession because I was now in business. I had to invest in my knowledge level to keep up with rising PT students and practicing professionals. I chose to advance my career by going back to school. In 2007, I enrolled in the doctorate program for Physical Therapy at Alabama State University.

How important is Expertise to a company or organization?

ESTABLISH PRINCIPLES

CEO: Able to act decisively regarding; human, financial, environmental and technical challenges that face a corporation. The CEO must ultimately make sure the organization is constantly improving through a structured approach, in line with owner orientation to risk/reward.

CFO: Responsible for the oversight, management, and leadership in the areas of global finance, internal control, auditing, and materials management. This is accomplished by overseeing financial and accounting system controls and standards, leading and directing the finance department, maintaining financial health of the organization and participation in strategic planning. This person also provides strategic consultation regarding business prioritization, resource allocation and all financial issues.

Chief Operations Officer (COO), corporate officer: Manages the day-to-day activities of the corporation. The COO reports directly to the chief executive officer and is one of the highest-ranking members of an organization. The COO is assisted by the senior vice president. The COO is also responsible for operations management (OM). The focus of the COO is towards strategic, tactical, and short-term OM, which means they are responsible for design, operation, and improvement of systems that create and deliver solutions and services. Managers need to understand the real work behind company core operations, and the COO's primary concern is operations improvement.

CIO, chief information officer: Primarily responsible for strategy development and execution, sales management, service development, public relations, marketing communications (including advertising and promotions), pricing, market research, and customer service. Compounded by day-to-day activities of these functions, which range from the highly analytical to highly creative advertising and promotions. The CIO is invariably reliant upon resources beyond their direct control. Priorities and/or resources of functional areas outside of marketing such as production, information technology, legal, and finance have a direct impact on the achievement of marketing objectives. Consequently, more than any other senior executive, the CIO must influence peers to achieve their own goals. Clearly, this necessity to lead peers compounds the complexity of challenge faced by the CIO.

TABLE 4 -
EXPERTISE EVALUATION TOOL

Complete table and totals to collect assessment.
Check the box of the "Yes" Column if the evaluation point applies to your organiza-
tion; Check the box of the "No" in the box if the evaluation point does not apply to your
organization. Each "Yes" answer is worth 1.0 points, record the value in the - Point
Value column. Add points in the Point Value column.

EXPERTISE EVALUATION POINTS	YES (1.0 pts for each answer)	NO (0 pts for each answer)	POINT VALUE
Human Capital - Subject Matter Experts?			
Best Practices – reliably sourced evidence based skills or techniques?			
Use of Qualitative methods?			
Incorporation of Research, Knowledge and Experiences - Application?			
Scale of Expertise?			
Self-Assurance?			
Authority & Resolve?			
Prioritizes resources and function?			
Development and Innovation influenced by specialization?			
Innovative and Application of technology have a superior approach?			
TOTAL – *Degree Potential x10*			

XPERIENCE

EXPERIENCE: *Skill or knowledge gained by doing something; direct observation of; practical knowledge skill or practice derived from direct observation.*

"Experience is the use of the perfect imperfections. Being innovative and so impressive that others want to imitate. The Ergo Way is not textbook and could be seen as unorthodox" — *Terrance Mickie, Human Resource Manager and Nurse Recruiter, Howard University Hospital*

How important is Experience to a company or organization? High-performing workplaces tend to have great open communication between staff and management. Having experience in communication is essential to training, team work, and meetings. A high-performing workplace should have clear goals, a mission and vision statement. A mechanistic organization, with strict policy and procedures can limit ambiguity between staff, however, no position is undervalued, and all are held to high standards of excellence, producing distinction in service. A system of authority is fundamental to organization structure in a high-performing workplace, providing place and standard for great ethics and camaraderie. High performance environments also value diversity, community and the central values that lead practice and documented processes. Documenting processes allow new comers to perform with 'tribal-knowledge' and guidance of subject matter experts with minimal risk, while maintaining high expectations for production, customer satisfaction and internal communication.

The experienced workplace should be led by a team of identified experienced executives or a collaboration of specialized experienced teams and groups that enhance and foster development.

"The Method of Science" by Colquitt, Lepine and Wesson describes the theory of job satisfaction, stress, motivation and encouragement. Job satisfaction is essential to personal growth and development in a workplace.

The method starts with a critical question and empirical thinking, answering these questions:

- What leads to a high-performance team?
- What organizations can we draw from that are considered high-performing?

- What is the latest research on high-performing organizations?
- Who is the authority on the topic?

EXERCISE:

Use the questions to draw a hypothesis or statement, and in process to develop the statement, think on factors that lead to a building a high-performance team. Be certain and consider the course of action required by the factor (or characteristic) and how following through in the action will lead to a productive team. Expect that the factors will be relative to one another, and specialized to each area of corporate organization. The factors should apply to all parts of the company and the way they are applied to a part of organizational structure may require specific human resources, operations and financial specializations. Keep note of your answers and factors for use as you develop and gain experiences.[xvi]

The article "Linking Capacities of High Quality Relationships to Team Learning and Performance in Service" by Daphna Brueller and Abraham Carmeli detail the importance of team relationship by connecting high-quality relationships with the strength of the intrateam. The article states, "Executives and managers behaviors and actions provide the conditions for improved learning, processes, thereby cultivating competitive advantages in the workplace and ultimately enhancing the viability of the organization."[xvii] The article highlights the factors that are internal and external for team development. They directly relate to team learning and trainings developed in the organization. The benefits of positive associations within the organization are necessary for the performance of the functioning of the organization. Build positive relationships with every customer, every employee and believe a person works best in a healthy environment.

Structure is the experience framework around which the group is organized—the underpinnings which keep the coalition, functioning. It is the operating manual that tells members how the organization is put together and how it works. More specifically, structure describes how members are accepted, how experienced leadership is chosen, and how experienced decisions are made.

Operations are dependent on the efforts, abilities, and experience of personnel, professionals, and management.

How valuable is employee development? Develop talent. Focus experiences on corporate goals and look at what contributed most to professional development over the time. Experience is gauge to ability to assess, search, train, teach, and assist. The successor can grow executive talent into future leaders. There are strong suggestions to look for highly effective experienced people and broker talent across the organization. Avoid placing mediocre people in key positions.

In John Wooden's book on leadership traits, Skill, he encourages everyone to hone in on all skills and develop them into greater value by highlighting the experiences gained in the process. Recruit or develop people with the skill set and talents that can be of great utility; to their fullest potential.

TABLE 5 -
EXPERIENCE SWOT EVALUATION TOOL

Complete table and totals to collect assessment.
Check the box of the "Yes" Column if the evaluation point applies to your organization; Check the box of the "No" in the box if the evaluation point does not apply to your organization. Each "Yes" answer is worth 1.0 points, record the value in the - Point Value column. Add points in the Point Value column.

EXPERIENCE - SWOT - EVALUATION POINTS	YES (1.0 pts for each answer)	NO (0 pts for each answer)	POINT VALUE
Create educative processes of continual learning? Have educative processes of continual learning been created?			
Effective interaction? Have effective interaction measures been created/implemented?			
Are there clearly identified internal processes to resolve issues or complete action?			
Is there a plan of action for organizational reaction to adverse conditions?			
Adaptability – Able to change to market – Ready for change?			
Is the organization or are you prepared for future challenges and changes - Readiness?			
Is the organization or are you able to create or lead a high-performance team?			
Is the organization or are you able to gain perspective of other organizations and draw from their considerations?			

TABLE 5 - EXPERIENCE SWOT EVALUATION TOOL			
Has the organization or have you reviewed latest research on high-performing organizations?			
Does the organization or do you follow authority on topic?			
TOTAL – *Degree Potential x10*			

ETHICS

ETHICS: *What is morally good, a theory or system of moral value; guiding philosophy; Skill or knowledge gained by doing something; direct observation of; practical knowledge skill or practice derived from direct observation.*[xviii]

"Great service, price, and ethics enhances ... wealth and leadership." - *Gail Jernigan*

"Being ethical means being above board and being committed to being honest and truthful" - *Richard Flanagan, Human Resource Director Ergo Solutions*

How important are Ethics to a company or organization? A high standard of ethics is essential to success. The reputation of a company is in the hands of its employees. Each must maintain the highest ethical and professional standards. Basic honesty is key to ethical behavior. Trustworthiness in the marketplace is essential to building solid and lasting relationships with customers, vendors, and with others.

Here is an example of the 'Code of Ethics, describing standards a company may expect healthcare employees/staff to adhere to:

- Improves the quality of health care services
- Decreases costs: To detect and prevent any violations of statutes:
  - To monitor organization/provider adherence to applicable statutes and regulatory requirements
  - To assure that the appropriate operation policies and procedures are in place that demonstrate a provider/practice/healthcare institution's commitment to complying with the law
- Increases profitability.
- Provides structure: Formulation of effective internal controls; an increased likelihood of identifying and preventing unlawful and unethical behavior;
- Ability to quickly react to employee operational compliance concerns and effectively target resources to address those concerns
- Provide a mechanism to encourage employees to report potential problems and allow for appropriate internal inquiry and corrective action;
- Procedures that allow prompt & thorough investigation of misconduct – early detection

When applied to everyday business, acting ethically means adhering to law, competing with others in an honest manner, and performing daily tasks without any element of deceit. Many companies around the globe update "written codes of conduct as a result of past corporate scandals." It is not uncommon for a company to update this document on a yearly basis. After a code of conduct document has been updated, each staff member must read and understand the document. Further, all employees must adhere to the updated codes of conduct, and those that do not follow these regulations are often dismissed. Although managers must follow the same codes of conduct as employees, these individuals have additional obligations.

In high performance work systems, effective human resource practices are critical to the development of the organizational structure for success. The efforts of communication highly important to the functionality of specialized departments are "Increased with horizontal communication." It is encouraged that organizations and companies develop and maintain structures with 'flat hierarchies.'

"Power distance is the extent to which the member of the society accepts unequal distribution of power." Develop "low ratio of administrative to labor personnel to increase vertical communication throughout the organization."

By keeping a close and effectively managed team, organizations will experience "an increased emphasis on support and technical staff." Develop a system of relationship between departments forming high-performing organization "cross-functional and coordinated task forces."

TABLE 6 -
ETHICAL EVALUATION TOOL

Complete table and totals to collect assessment.
Check the box of the "Yes" Column if the evaluation point applies to your organiza-tion; Check the box of the "No" in the box if the evaluation point does not apply to your organization. Each "Yes" answer is worth 1.25 points, record the value in the - Point Value column. Add points in the Point Value column.

ETHICAL EVALUATION POINTS	YES (1.25 pts for each answer)	NO (0 pts for each answer)	POINT VALUE
Improves the quality of health care services?			
Decreases costs: To detect and prevent any violations of statutes?			
To monitor a healthcare organization/provider's adherence to applicable statutes and regulatory requirements?			
To assure that the appropriate operation policies and procedures are in place that demonstrates a provider/ practice/healthcare institution's commitment to complying with the law?			
Increases profitability and provides structure: formulation of effective internal controls; An increased likelihood of identifying and preventing unlawful and unethical behavior?			
Ability to quickly react to employee's operational compliance concerns and effectively target resources to address those concerns?			

TABLE 6 - ETHICAL EVALUATION TOOL			
Provide a mechanism to encourage employees to report potential problems and allow for appropriate internal inquiry and corrective action?			
Procedures that allow prompt & thorough investigation of misconduct – early detection?			
TOTAL – *Degree Potential x10*			

FULCRUM AS FLEXIBILITY

Purpose of Flexibility Training

I t is important to include flexibility training as part of your clients' regular fitness routines. Improved flexibility may enhance performance in aerobic training and muscular conditioning as well as in sport. There is scientific evidence that the incidence of injury decreases when people include flexibility training in their routines due to the enhanced ability to move unimpeded through a wider range of motion (ROM). The only exception to this would be when there is an excessive or unstable ROM, which may increase the likelihood of injury. When used appropriately, flexibility training allows clients to become more in tune with their body.

In business it is likewise important to have flexibility — the ability to be in tune within the business. An assessment of this section will encourage you and your company to solicit subjective information from your clients, customers, patients, employees, managers, executives and stakeholders. These areas are the flexibility of the business. Anywhere there is immobility, it is important to increase and improve flexibility. The following six areas must be strengthened with exercise. Ergo Solutions E-Words for Administration and Management Flexibility are:

mpowerment

ndorsement

ffort (endeavor)

ssentials

quity

conomics

# MPOWERMENT

EMPOWERMENT: *To give official authority or power to. To promote the self-actualization or influence of.*[xix]

"The Ergo way invites strengthening from within, with creativity and technical ability. The Ergo Way asks what else can be brought to the vision and future. Empowerment is the viability of a company, its potency, strength, and power to perform...to have viable resource capital." - *Michael McFadden, Author, Minister, Compliance Officer*

"People who can think, think for themselves and go through the mechanics to do it. Promoting up." - *Henry Vaughn, Capitol Hill Hospital*

As a novice therapist starting out after graduation from PT school, I learned early about empowerment in the workplace. I had the benefit of working under the leadership of a mentor/friend, Jeff Wright. Under his leadership I was empowered to become a leader among my peers through training, teaching and being coached up. I was empowered to make minimal decisions, take small risks in a learning and teaching environment. This allowed me to make my mistakes and grow with a supervisor willing to coach me. I learned techniques by listening, management by training and administration by watching. I learned through reading that there is a "perception of empowerment" among multi-disciplinary team members.

This perception of empowerment fostered a comfortable environment for me to grow. My first five years of practice was a mental roller coaster. I had to decide whether to stay a PT or change professions; face the challenges and see them as worth more than my paycheck. Pay day would come and I would still want to quit. I lost focus and drive for my profession and I wavered to stay in it. I was bored; I felt like I had mastered the practice and saw no growth potential. What changed my mind? I had great leadership and I accepted their leadership. I had supervisors and directors over the years especially, Dawn Cooper. She shared tools that empowered me to love my profession. I read that "examining perceptions of empowerment is warranted for organizational commitment among physical therapy staff." Dawn Cooper's leadership encouraged me to understand and investigate empowerment within our department.

Kanter's theory provides a theoretical framework for "empowerment within organizations." It suggests that an organizational structure ought to provide "access to information, support, resources, opportunity, and formal and informal power." I liked the idea that I had informal power to make trial attempts in my profession to find my passion and the drive to keep me from "the pitfalls." I felt empowered by other mature professionals - in PT - who encouraged me to do what I loved and that was to teach, train, and coach others. When I had the opportunity to do this I felt I could be me every day. When I can motivate others, I can - ABSOLUTELY - be me every day. My mentors/friends truly nurtured me to lead.

As a PT, licensed in the District of Columbia, I have witnessed the great health disparities in the lower income wards of the city. I have been empowered and driven to be a catalyst for change in the Wards 5, 7 and 8. My personal perspective comes from growing up in Philadelphia, Pennsylvania, a similar urban city whose residents experienced health disparities in low-income neighborhoods as well. I chose physical therapy because of the ability to make change in individual's lives through healing. My experience with Mr. Wright and Ms. Cooper empowered me through my 21st year as a professional, with dedication to the profession. I was encouraged by my mentors to act, to keep my zeal and to be led by my passion to address the health disparities that exists in my community in D.C. through excellence in care in positive environments of PT; by focusing my professional growth to include the ethical causes I cared about and to build programs that allowed me to address the needs of the community as a professional.

Empowerment to act as an expert transforms the individual, especially at work, into persons who can carry on the focus, function and ideals of business, ensuring business can go forward without halting services to find a subject matter expert. I carry this concept with me as a business owner to empower others around me. Empowerment is vital to developing in your business and organization.

How important is Empowerment to a company or organization? Training departments must empower staff to be highly functional. "Emotional Intelligence" - handling emotions effectively in the workplace. These five areas highlight the need for emotional intelligence in the workplace.

- Self-awareness.
- Managing emotions.
- Motivating others.
- Showing empathy.
- Staying connected.

Be aware and practice to identify all to maintain a productive organization. Empowering and promoting these areas to enhance service provision will yield quality care to clients/patients in every facility.

Self-awareness is essential to realistic self-assessment. Empower managers to train staff members to heightened self-awareness. Provide staff with feedback on strengths and weaknesses on an individual basis so that staff interaction with clients/customers is improved daily. As part of our service model we provide annual assessments of each employee. During these evaluations, we rate their coping and self-management skills. Self-awareness is essential for each therapist.

Our executive management team is particularly unique; we truly empathize with staff therapists, as each executive is also a therapist. "The ability to be in touch, as leaders, is key to making sure employees follow leadership. Showing empathy is essential to coaching.[xx]" Coaching empowers team building and development training experiences for less experienced therapists.

The ability to improve emotional intelligence, cope with and manage emotions, affects interaction with one another. Promotion of optimistic thinking from leaders, help them become more effective in their leadership through training and studying ways to develop emotional skills.

"Thought leadership," another empowerment tool, can be viewed as innovative, initiative, ideal, informal, and implementable. "Thought leadership is the championing of new ideas."

INNOVATIVE

The Thought Leader – the ones who innovates from the bottom to the top which is contrary to top to the bottom theory = "essential for success." Legendary Coach John Wooden, of UCLA basketball, designed a success pyramid, he used for coaching leadership and taught it to other coaches, but it is a definitive character-building tool. His 'Traits of the leader' which can be applied to all are essential reading for every leader of every type. Coach Wooden believed that coaches can learn from players and that players have an empowered responsibility to be innovative on and off the courts. In the workplace, the employee should be invited to be innovative, using their talents and training to further address the mission of the company.

INITIATIVE

Thought leadership is inclusive of everyone because it empowers everyone to take ownership in the business, department and/or projects, etc. When people are empowered to make change and positive influence, they tend to make and take actions that follow the same. It is important that managers allow and plan for employees to take ownership of the role they have agreed to take on. "It can be shown by non-managerial employees, being a type of initiative." This will present as a great opportunity for employees to present input and show leadership. Stepping forward to take charge is not a power grab it is 'know-how' at work.

IDEA DRIVEN

Thought leadership is an idea driven from the bottom to the top. Each employee is empowered to initiate new ideas and bring to the forefront of the company leadership. The platform is picked up by the innovator to bring to fruition. Thought leadership is the "championing of new ideas rather than anything to do with managing people or helping a group achieve a goal." Being idea-driven encourages employees to keep their minds on the tasks at hand and to be solution-driven. This is different from where a governing body from the top comes up with all ideas and controls all its planning.

INFORMAL

Informal leadership, a label used to describe employees who take charge temporarily despite having no formal authority over anyone, gives employees charge over a project and/or idea. This differs from a more formal leadership structure where people are appointed or empowered to hold a position to carry out the job tasks.

IMPLEMENTIVE

"Thought leadership stops once the idea for change has been accepted. Implementation entails a journey from idea to outcome where thought leadership sells the tickets for the journey." *Thought leadership* allows the employee to have room to grow. It allows for maturation of the employees by having buy-in and seeing their projects to completion. By being open to ideas, top executives will create an atmosphere of inclusion in the workplace.

Thought leadership is led by influential employees that implement new ideas in an informal process, which can establish great outcomes. This approach is in contrast with leadership models that come from the top down, which often create feelings of exclusion felt throughout the work environment. Leadership teams should look at every level, so that everyone is included. Entry-level employees to senior management are more accepting of change when they know their voices are heard and feel empowered to share their ideas.

TABLE 7 -
◢MPOWERMENT EVALUATION TOOL

Complete table and totals to collect assessment.
Check the box of the "Yes" Column if the evaluation point applies to your organiza-
tion; Check the box of the "No" in the box if the evaluation point does not apply to your
organization. Each "Yes" answer is worth 1.25 points, record the value in the - Point
Value column. Add points in the Point Value column.

EMPOWERMENT EVALUATION POINTS	YES (1.25 pts for each answer)	NO (0 pts for each answer)	POINT VALUE
Innovative?			
Initiative?			
Ideal?			
Informal?			
Implementable?			
The need for self-awareness?			
Managing emotions?			
Motivating others?			
Showing empathy?			
Staying connected and requiring organization?			
TOTAL – *Degree Potential x10*			

# ENDORSEMENT

ENDORSEMENT: *Public or official statement in support or approval.*

As a senior therapist I learned the importance of endorsement, but I had to grow as a professional to really understand how endorsement worked in the workplace. How I present myself every day in the workplace is called professionalism. I am endorsing myself in the way I dress, my attitude, and how I perform, in everything I do I represent the company that I work for. I matured to a senior therapist; began working at Greater Southeast Hospital. I grew in my professional behavior, learning from others in the profession – some managers, some directors. I decided to focus my passions to become a leader in management at the hospital. In that process, I realized that gaining endorsement from others would take time. At first, I was denied opportunities to lead, and to be frank, I wasn't ready, and it showed: I failed to gain endorsements or win the buy-in (the backing) of others. It took more time than I wanted and for a while, it was frustrating. I felt underappreciated, disrespected and wanted to change jobs – leave the hospital. It seemed that my advancement in the profession was limited in that place.

Developing as a professional and exhibiting the behavior expected from a person in my position began an adversity for me. I was frustrated by the stagnant plane I was on. Professionally, I was in a lull. Going through the motions as required and discouraged by my leadership, I needed a professional boost, an energy recharge. To give myself the platform I needed, I decided to invest in myself. I sought disciple and development as a professional, so meet the call of my industry to elevate my level of expertise, I went after my doctorate degree.

In 2010, I graduated with my doctorate in Physical therapy from Alabama State University; 15 years after earning my bachelors of science degree from Florida A &M University in 1995. After gaining my doctorate, the governing board of Physical Therapy, the American Physical Therapy Association (APTA), endorsed me in the "2020 Vision Statement for Physical Therapy."

Being endorsed by the organization that sets the standards my colleagues and I are regulated, guided and measured by, I was profoundly encouraged to be guided by integrity, life-long learning, and a commitment to comprehensive and accessible health programs for all people.

Specifically, I was endorsed by the APTA to provide "culturally sensitive care distinguished by trust, respect, and an appreciation for individual differences." I was charged to learn and develop in new technologies: Clinical research, direct patient/ client care and to foster growth of the physical therapy profession. I advanced my career as a doctor of PT to work toward conformity and compliance through development, promotion, and adherence to practicing standards using best evidence approaches. The APTA has endorsed physical therapists to be entrepreneurs. It endorses autonomy while encouraging positive networking in a "multidisciplinary health care model."

In business, positive endorsement of professionalism to perfect branding of self and in developing a spirit of owning an entrepreneurship in practice is very important. This must be offered as an endorsement to all professionals – taking time to ensure individuals are empowered to act and endorsed as experts leads flexibility and personal growth in the workplace as a professional.

How important is Endorsement to a company or organization? From Kotler and Keller - "the added value given to our service, which reflects the way our consumers think, feel, and act with respect to the brand. They suggest the advantages of strong brands are improved perceptions of service, greater loyalty, less vulnerability to competitive marketing actions, less crises, larger margins, greater trade cooperation, increased marketing communication effectiveness and licensing opportunities."

Endorsement of brand promise sets a vision for what "the brand must be and do for consumers."

BRANDING

Kotler and Keller suggest that branding can "identify influential individuals and companies and devote extra effort to them, supply key people with product samples, work through community influential, and develop word-of-mouth referral channels to build business." Strong brands equal endorsement advantage: "Larger margins; more inelastic consumer response to price increases; more elastic consumer response to price decreases."

We realize the importance of "increasing our shelf presence and dependency, attracting customers seeking variety, increasing competition in the firm, and yielding economics on advertising, sales, and service." Our portfolio examines the brand dynamic pyramid to build a strong brand relationship within each of our facilities. We have emphasized the importance of moving from just a presence to having true relevance in the community, by quality performance and providing the advantage of the best practices to ultimately develop a bond of trust. At Stoddard Baptist, Lisner Home and Specialty Hospital of Washington we tested how the relationship with the customer is important to retention of contract. To familiarize our concept, we posted flyers with the Brand-Dynamic Pyramid in the facilities. We measured "branding auditing, branding tracking and valuations. We manage brand equity with reinforcement, revisitation and crises."

Our team approach beats out our competition, time after time. Our advantage is that most of us previously worked for "foreign" companies. Armed with a passion for service to our community, we maintain and cultivate organic relationships in the community where we do business. We work where we live, we build where we work, and we participate in community development to ensure the future of our community. We endorse our community as worthy of our tax dollars, our service and future endeavors.

We know of many rehab companies, based outside of our community and locality – for example from Midwest or Southern states, who have assumed contracts in our community. We have seen these relationships produce new opportunities for our company: Our competitors experience loss of relationship with area nursing homes because of proximity – Where a great part of service is perception of immediate resolution of customer concerns. Immediate response is hallmark to our service model of success for clinical, administrative, regulatory and financial issues.

Ergo Solutions as a brand repays response to all our customers; this simple action beats our competition. The Ergo way means that when a facility in our service scope needs prompt service, we are there in provision, service, intelligence and fortitude. We are service-driven, to produce for the customer, while balancing supply and demand and staying in contact with the customer."

According to Kotler and Keller, brand valuation is "the job of estimating the total financial value of the brand."

BRAND RESONANCE PYRAMID

The pyramid builds upon "the brand identity to having meaning and having a response to how you feel about the product and then building a relationship with the product or service. As the customer ascends the pyramid toward

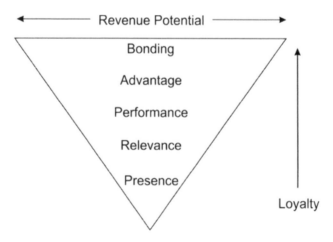

Figure 1: The Brand Resonance Pyramid – Model by M. Brown

relation the effect grows from deep and broad feelings to a more positive and intense feeling.

Kotler and Keller share Bedbury's eight principles: "(1) relying on brand awareness has become marketing fool's gold; (2) you have to know it before you can grow it; (3) always remember the Spandex rule of brand extension; (4) great brands establish enduring customer relationships; (5) everything matters; (6) all brands need good parents; (7) big is no excuse for being bad; and, (8) relevance, simplicity, and humanity."

As shared previously; "brand equity is the added value endowed to products and services" and "strong brands have the advantage of less vulnerability to competitive marketing actions:

- Improved perceptions of product performance.
- Greater loyalty.
- Less vulnerability to competitive marketing actions.
- Less vulnerability to marketing crises.
- Larger margins.
- More inelastic consumer response to price increases.
- More elastic consumer response to price decreases.
- Greater trade cooperation and support.
- Increased marketing communications effectiveness.
- Possible licensing opportunities.
- Additional brand extension opportunities."

These are all areas in which we can win for our customers.

Other ways companies find advantage in strong endorsement is via social media, video and mobile phones. The idea of developing, managing and maintaining an endorsement portfolio is critical to doing business today. Being able to establish strong endorsing relationships in social media; create a following, and cultivate it. The Brand Dynamic pyramid suggests that the following steps (in ascending order) are essential in building strong relationships: (1) presence, (2) relevance, (3) performance, (4) advantage, and (5) bonding."

"The endorsement is the logic of competitive advantage that intersects a strong brand, innovation and existing ideas." — Frans Johannsen 'Diversity Drives Innovation and Growth"

TABLE 8 -
ENDORSEMENT EVALUATION TOOL

Complete table and totals to collect assessment.
Check the box of the "Yes" Column if the evaluation point applies to your organiza-
tion; Check the box of the "No" in the box if the evaluation point does not apply to your
organization. Each "Yes" answer is worth 1.25 points, record the value in the - Point
Value column. Add points in the Point Value column.

ENDORSEMENT EVALUATION POINTS	YES (1.25 pts for each answer)	NO (0 pts for each answer)	POINT VALUE
Using tools for effective branding?			
Study presentation, position, representation, and perspective?			
Identified association to market			
Presence - Campaign unique to market?			
Relevance?			
Performance?			
Advantage?			
Bonding?			
TOTAL – *Degree Potential x10*			

FFORT

ENDORSEMENT: *Work done, a serious attempt to do something; conscience exertion of power.*

"The Ergo Way is difficult to see as effort. I will say it's more "effervescent" because your team has fun while working. You get great mileage out of the company, management and staff." - *Remy Johnson, DCHCA 2013 Administrator of the year, Stoddard Baptist Nursing Home*

"Effort is the true testament of challenge. It's the closest link to positive outcomes otherwise 'Symbiotic'." - *Matt and Ron Longo, Owners of Mid-Atlantic Prosthetics and Orthotics*

As a manager in the profession for over 18 years I learned the importance of work. Sometime people say I wish I did what you do. I must chuckle or laugh sometimes because friends and family think that my job is plush or sweet. As a manager of Lisner Louise Dickson Hurt Home in Washington, D.C., a 60-bed skilled nursing home and 40-bed assisted living facility, the days may have seemed slow.

However, the demand for rehab service was always acute and greatly needed. I found myself doing both clinical and administrative work. The work day of a therapist requires most of us to want to nap or rest when we get off. The work day as a therapist is filled with transfers, gait training, exercising clients, documentation, meetings, and addressing all customer needs and wants. When I became a manager, I realized how stressful it could be dealing with staff and placing demands of productivity on departments that I managed.

As a manager I learned to work smart in my efforts. I realized that I whistle while I work. Well, if you ever worked with or under me you know that I sing most of the day. The singing allows me to be me. I enjoy the profession of PT because it allows me to encourage my patients, clients and those around me in song. I have been doing this for my whole career and most tend to tell me the same thing: "Keep your day job!"

I take this as a compliment when they say stick to my day job because I believe I am good at my day job. To be a highly effective therapist in the workplace, it is important to strategize work efforts towards getting the job done and tasks completed. As a manager, I expect positive work effort from my team. I do this by empowering them to be flexible in their productivity.

At the Lisner Home, I learned that being flexible in management meets the needs of the customer. I take this as an important factor in running your own business. It is critical that effort is relevant to business.

In business, I learned to encourage and empower managers to consider traditional thinking and value it in comparison to the systems suggested by postmodern experts. The role of a highly effective 'manager' is dynamic today in business. Internally, we implement ways to encourage managers to accept responsibility by defining the roles of the corporate authorities set in place to manage staff, focusing efforts to increase productivity, improve performance and identify problems or blockers to solve or remove.

The efforts that empower a manager must include assigning the role of revenue oversight as realizing cost is essential to every company. Manager ability and freedom to effectively analyze trends and execute forecast futures for a company must represent the goals of the company and be evaluated from several schools of thought. Economic and fiscal responsibility requires managers to prepare reports and statements to be reviewed by ownership, leadership, and other managers. These data collections clarify the present state of the company. Each manager migrates to leadership to be an effective part of the organization.

The efforts of a manager direct their area of authority. The systems thinking approach that changes how managers should modify the way they see themselves in their role as manager. The transition from worker to manager is explained and in the "analogy of an accomplished violinist moving to being a conductor." Emphasizes a "change of attitude and habits" to motivate and empower others. The manager is thought to go through "transformation of professional identity." This concept identifies and inspires the effectiveness in development of the efforts.

As a manager, I also learned synthesis and analysis in different ways of thinking towards problems and the organization. Our efforts are directed to solve problems for our customers and patients. We implement leadership through positive energy and commitment by learning three skills as a "futurist, a strategist and integrator." These skills present a way of thinking that present opportunity to learn from trends and current events, preparing a manager to execute for future growth and development: The Ergo Way. The role of the Ergo manager is to empower and endorse positive "ideas, beliefs and emotions for the common objectives" in leadership.

In John Seddons' *Six Steps to Improving Productivity*, the role of the Ergo manager is further defined. It starts with thinking about the customer, "knowledge of the customer, their attitude, habits and their efforts to design products and services." Seddon suggests systems thinking versus the top-down approach. Systems thinking empowers managers to focus on perspective and improving "outbound transactions," things like marketing, sales, invoicing and most delivery of services and goods. Seddon suggests in *Fit for the Future*, to be within "capable measures" to meet demand and maintain value with the customer. In *Think Flow* the role of the manager to system thinking is essential to "core processing." The Ergo manager monitors rework and duplication and sees the system through inspection of any "bottlenecking, black holes, botching or filtering." In the article *This Means Me* the role of manager is challenged to take ownership and take on a new attitude and energy towards the customer; focusing on excellence. This way of thinking, sees the manager as a part of the integrated system and makes sure the company ideas are included in every process.

In business I learned that the definition of the manager's role has less to do with the mindset of the manager and is more focused on the effort of the manager. I appreciated the value of these articles to change the way of thinking about the role of the manager to effectively meet the need of the system. We endeavor to engage each manager as a human being first, considering the emotional and intellectual parts of the manager.

It will continue to require the manager to be trained to think positively and with synergy. The psychological aspect of The Ergo Way asks the manager to commit to "learning, develop interpersonal judgment, gain self-knowledge, and coping with stress and emotions." The idea is that, the manager should not just assume the position but develop an enterprising way of thinking to "improve services, reduce costs, and increase the probability that customers will continue" with the employee/client relationship in business. The Ergo manager should continue to "focus on purpose of business excellence and eradicate busyness.

How important is Effort to a company or organization? Develop marketing efforts and strategy to influence change, promotion, pricing and presentation. Fit expectations of potential audience: Clients, Partners, Employees, Customers, etc. Create a conscience exertion in to marketing Information System. In promoting changes, focus company efforts on-line, in the community, conferences, and educational opportunities. Build a diverse plan of marketing to differing demographics. It is critical to recognize a rapidly changing market. For example, one effort may be to update websites to meet appeal, speak to all audiences, identify types of accounts, businesses, organizations and institutions. Understand, traditional efforts are long gone. Change to take advantage of the changing market. To achieve advanced expansion, efforts should focus on new opportunities.

In the healthcare industry, we all face the same marketing challenges, no matter how big or small.

Our strategy: *Be an expert.*

Develop these 5 things:
- Knowledge
- Training
- Study/Continued Education
- Craft/Specialty
- Skills

TABLE 9 -
EFFORT EVALUATION TOOL

Complete table and totals to collect assessment.
Check the box of the "Yes" Column if the evaluation point applies to your organization; Check the box of the "No" in the box if the evaluation point does not apply to your organization. Each "Yes" answer is worth 2.0 points, record the value in the - Point Value column. Add points in the Point Value column.

EFFORT EVALUATION POINTS	YES (2.0 pts for each answer)	NO (0 pts for each answer)	POINT VALUE
Knowledge?			
Training?			
Study/Continued Education?			
Craft/Specialty?			
Skills?			
TOTAL – Degree Potential x10			

SSENTIALS

ESSENTIALS: *A thing that is necessary; first principles.*

The essentials help achieve the desired results to "process flow and improvements related to quality, cost, and delivery." - *Atwater*

As a director of Rehab services in more than five facilities in the DC area, I have learned the importance of the essentials. Working as director of rehabilitation at Grant Park Care Center and Lorton Prison, I learned to work with very little equipment; I was given minimal resources and had to work in scarcity.

It was frustrating because we didn't have ideal equipment and what we did have was outdated, but we made it work. We used what we had. We worked with the essentials to provide the best care to a group of people who truly needed our specialized and quality care.

Knowing the essentials or basics that enabled my team to provide service created for us a 'break-even point' to use as a marker. Our practice to function and know the essentials produced longevity and continuity in our business.

In 2001 my partners and I embraced from potential investors a concept - that owners should evaluate their own personal characteristics, background, and motivations to stay in business. As a director, I evaluated my motivation, support and feedback, experience, knowledge, and skills in that mid- management position. Even before becoming a business owner, as a director leading a staff of up to 15 therapists, I had to evaluate my essential or crucial capacities. I needed to make sure I maintained the ability, capacity and skills to provide those things essential to management and administration. To cover this perspective, we evaluated ourselves using the **FINHOP** assessment tool. This acronym stands for **F**inance, **I**nformation **M**anagement, **N**etworking, **H**uman resource management, **O**perations and **P**lanning and strategy. These aptitudes, skills and scopes were not a part of my Physical Therapy curriculum in school. I realized that these essentials were required for leadership in management and business ownership for me would give me the trajectory I needed to advance my business knowledge, skills and ability. To that end, I enrolled in the MBA program at the University of Maryland University College and graduated in 2013.

How important are essentials to a company or organization? System thinking benefits overall business, with increased market share and profits. From Michael Gerber, *The E-Myth Revisited* describes the idea of creating systems and having the systems run the business, to position a business to prepare for growth.

Establishing a system creates automatic, basic practices as standard process. This removes human error and creates ability to maintain and manage a high level of excellence over an extended period.

Essentials establish synergy and focus across all principles. Management can create an engaged and empowered workforce where continuous improvement is aligned with strategies and customer needs, resulting in long-term profitability, growth and customer satisfaction.

Innovation is vital to business intelligence, vested through formal training, study and expertise.

Quick note on Systems: When designing a system, include a reinforcing loop, (this technique is used very often by program coders and data miners), so that the system is viewed as a tool and the improvements achieved by using the system become associated to specific, results. Tools help achieve desired results, and with experience, understanding and appreciation, tools are refined. Understand that the true value of a system is gained when it may be used for more that production, finding greater use to analyze data for research and development, purchasing, and other business processes. When this is achieved a team transitions to the Systems level.

SYSTEMS VIEW

The system view is a specific collection and arrangement of tools used together to achieve a smooth material flow through a specific production process. From this vantage point, managers can connect the dots between a process flow and improvements related to quality, cost, and delivery. Although the systems view is limited, the benefits reaped are huge related to overall business results, such as increased market share and profits.

PRINCIPLE VIEW

There is the explicit understanding and agreement on the guiding principles of operational excellence. Atwater identified the following principles and the long-term effects of each:

- Create value for the customer – achieve purpose of the business
- Create constancy of purpose – generates synergy across the enterprise.
- Think systematically – generates synergy across the enterprise

- Focus on process
    - Embrace scientific thinking
    - Flow and pull value.
    - Process - create a continuous improvement in the environment.
    - Assure quality at the source.
    - Seek perfection.
- Lead with humility.
- Respect every individual

The above principles are universal and timeless beliefs that can be applied to all businesses. If managers focus on some principles and not all, some benefits will be seen but eventually improvement will become stagnant and decline. By establishing synergy and focus across all principles, management can create an engaged and empowered workforce and culture where continuous improvement is aligned with strategies and customer needs, resulting in long-term profitability, growth and customer satisfaction.

TABLE 10 - ESSENTIALS EVALUATION TOOL

Complete table and totals to collect assessment.
Check the box of the "Yes" Column if the evaluation point applies to your organization; Check the box of the "No" in the box if the evaluation point does not apply to your organization. Each "Yes" answer is worth 1.25 points, record the value in the - Point Value column. Add points in the Point Value column.

ESSENTIALS EVALUATION POINTS	YES (1.25 pts for each answer)	NO (0 pts for each answer)	POINT VALUE
Creating value for the customer – achieve purpose of the business?			
Create constancy of purpose – generates synergy across the enterprise?			
Think systematically – generates synergy across the enterprise?			
Focus on process?			
Embrace scientific thinking?			
Flow and pull value?			
Assure quality at the source?			
Seek perfection?			
TOTAL – *Degree Potential x10*			

QUITY

EQUITY: *Fairness or justice in the way people are treated.*

BRAND EQUITY

As a chief officer in Ergo Solutions I realized the importance of equity and developing brand image. I realized the importance of which information should be packaged to express who we are in business. In my office, I manage networking, information management and strategy & planning. This was a position that I received once we opened the doors as Ergo Solutions. I completed most efforts by trial and error. I do mean trial and error and many errors. I recall making our first marketing packets and when I look back at the work I did in 2001-2005, I just have to laugh because I did what I knew. My partners and I managed to brand Ergo Solutions with business cards, brochures, packets, websites and more that were remedial or novice at best.

Many people joked as we did not even spell our company name correctly for the first few years of existence. We had to make changes to our brand to match the excellence we provide as therapists.

Our brand was 'cheesy' but sincere to who we were at the time. Our genuine hearts, care, compassion and enthusiasm as therapists helped us propel the company.

My office expanded and got better when I invested in graphic designers, marketing experts, web designers, and a marketing committee of executives who changed the brand of Ergo Solutions. The brand of Ergo has transformed over a 10-year period to be more effective in marketing by planning and strategizing as a team.

I realized I should build equity within my team by empowering their creativity and innovation. I wanted my team members to feel ownership. The brand of Ergo and its value is credited to a team effort.

How important is Equity to a company or organization? Branding has emerged as a high management priority in the last decade due to the growing realization that brands are one of the most valuable intangible assets that firms have. Driven in part by this intense industry interest, academic researchers have explored many different brand-related topics in recent years, generating scores of papers, articles, research reports, and books. Here we identify some of the influential work in the branding area, highlighting what has been gathered academically regarding brand positioning, brand integration, brand-equity measurement, brand growth, and brand management. We should be careful to note that there are gaps that exist in the research of branding and brand equity and formulate a series of related research questions, related to:

- Choice modeling implications of the branding concept.
- Challenges of incorporating main interaction effects of branding.
- Impact of competition.

Employer branding represents firm efforts to promote within and outside the firm, a clear view of what makes it different and desirable as an employer. In recent years employer branding has gained popularity among practicing managers. Combining a resource-based view with brand equity[xxi] theory; exploring the relationship between employer branding and organizational career management[xxii]. The goal is to develop employer branding as a useful organizing framework for strategic human resource management.

TABLE 11 - EQUITY EVALUATION TOOL

Complete table and totals to collect assessment.
Check the box of the "Yes" Column if the evaluation point applies to your organization;
Check the box of the "No" in the box if the evaluation point does not apply to your organization. Each "Yes" answer is worth 2.5 points, record the value in the - Point Value column. Add points in the Point Value column.

EQUITY EVALUATION POINTS	YES (2.5 pts for each answer)	NO (0 pts for each answer)	POINT VALUE
Choice modeling implications of the branding concept?			
Challenges of incorporating main?			
Interaction effects of branding?			
Impact of competition?			
TOTAL – Degree Potential x10			

ECONOMICS

ECONOMICS: *The Process or system by which goods and services are produced, sold, and bought.*

The accounting information is used for budgetary purposes, calculating the profitability of potential proposals, calculating the profitability of potential resource candidates supporting our claims when collecting money from clients, explaining the variances when we receive invoices from contract companies with errors in them, ad hoc requests, etc..." - *Eddie Lovius*

How important are Economics to a company or organization? As an owner and principal of Ergo Solutions and Ergo OccMed I have learned economics from my partners Dr. Olu Ezeani and George Brownlee, PT. To ensure our organization is wise, informed and building our resources, we hired proficient account managers to help us manage finance. It is very important that finances are spoken about, reported and understood from all perspectives of the organization.

In business it's important to take account and 'mind' corporate economic approach of spending and use of resources between administrative offices. Economics of the company can work like a well-oiled machine when all offices are managed well. Learning to be good stewards of resources is a shared responsibility among officers in the company. I cooperate with Dr. Courtland Wyatt for operations leadership, Dr. Ezeani for financial leadership and George Brownlee for informational leadership.

In economics the "CFOs can help to enhance financial services by ensuring software functionality, directing documentation audits, determining charges are within market range, and establishing a productivity model for service."

I have learned from our finance team to pay attention to the details of finance by having a weekly meeting and monitoring finances. "It is imperative to adopt a reasonable standard of productivity, and have a staffing model to meet the demands for services. Managers should be able to pay close attention to the staffing mix for providing adequate service to the patient volume. It has been suggested that "Incremental changes in physical therapy can result in dramatic financial outcomes but attention to detail is required to discover where the opportunity exists.

Doing this will enhance the quality of services provided and strengthen your organizations bottom line."

Economists, Kotler and Keller suggest "going-rate pricing" is when "small firms follow the leader, changing prices when the market leader's prices change." We started in a well-established industry with the likes of Genesis Rehab, Aegis Therapies, Centennial, Paragon, Health South, Beverly Therapies, and other national powers. In pricing our services, we do not under sell our services, so we looked to the industry standards in rehab services. As a small firm we followed the lead of Aegis Therapies for Medicare Part A and B, and Medicaid case mix. Facilities often award companies by its service models along with the best prices. To compete with national powers, our pricing must be competitive.

Secondly, Kotler and Keller suggest "value pricing is not just setting lower prices; it is a matter of reengineering the company's operations to become a low-cost producer without sacrificing quality.

Ergo Solutions can adjust in setting lower pricing than competitors - due in part - to having a smaller operation and overhead. We can present fair prices for services to nursing homes and hospitals and remain profitable. Ergo Solutions can set a range for expecting return for services with the value-pricing strategy.

Thirdly and lastly, Kotler and Keller suggest for target-return pricing there is a "Break-Even Chart for Determining Target- Return Price and Break-Even Volume." Our finance team always establishes a break even analysis for service costs and expenses. In doing do, Ergo can set a target return for contribution margins in comparison to overhead costs. Ergo Solutions sets a standard for 40% return above the cost. The profit ratio expects is 1.4 for each facility. The established target can influence our pricing for services in each case mix for Medicare part A, Medicare part B and Medicaid.

Ergo Solutions can take the units at 18-20 and multiply by 1.4 to determine how much we choose to charge per outpatient, Medicaid or Medicare Part B. In patient requires determinant factors to establish the RUG rates to increase by 1.4 for at minimal 40% increase from the category from Low through to Ultra High. Ergo Solutions provides consultation to nursing homes and hospitals for a percentage of the reimbursed service the facility billed for under our care. The percentages are to establish a win-win situation for Ergo Solutions and the contracted facility.

Kotler and Keller suggest that "effective designing and implementing pricing strategies requires a thorough understanding of consumer pricing psychology and a systematic approach to setting, adapting, and changing prices." Ergo Solutions has a service model that cares for the customer's financial concerns that effect how we set pricing for services. We can adjust -make room- for negotiation to win an awarded contract. The consumer psychology is a big factor in comparison of competitive companies like Ergo Solutions to Aegis, Genesis, and Flagship. We can adapt prices to better the competition and make effective change. The ultimate desire is to win the contract and remain profitable for our rehab services.

Kotler and Keller suggest that a company pay attention to "the three major considerations in price setting: The customer's assessment, the costs and the competitor's prices." Ergo Solutions can consider pricing ultimately by due diligence and learning about the customer's need and desired results of rehab services. The setting of cost takes in consideration the payer sources but also the cost and expenses incurred by salaries, overhead and variable costs. Ergo Solutions also considers customers' prices if we are privy to that confidential information. Most times the customer will let us know if we are in or out of the ball park with the established figures.

TABLE 12 - ECONOMICS EVALUATION TOOL

Complete table and totals to collect assessment.
Check the box of the "Yes" Column if the evaluation point applies to your organization; Check the box of the "No" in the box if the evaluation point does not apply to your organization. Each "Yes" answer is worth 1.66 points, record the value in the - Point Value column. Add points in the Point Value column.

ECONOMICS EVALUATION POINTS	YES (1.66 pts for each answer)	NO (0 pts for each answer)	POINT VALUE
Accurate records retention?			
Financial analysis?			
Loan applications?			
IRS audits?			
Report creation?			
Obvious Return on Investment?			
TOTAL – *Degree Potential x10*			

MOVEMENT ARM AS MOBILITY IN BUSINESS
Purpose of Mobilization

Joint mobilization involves loosening up the restricted joint and increasing its range of motion by providing slow velocity and increasing amplitude movement directly into the barrier of a joint, moving the actual bone surfaces on each other in ways patients cannot move the joint themselves.

In business it is likewise to have mobility. The optimal functional capacity of the business requires careful mobilization and amplitude in administrative and management activity. An assessment of this section will encourage you and your company to solicit subjective information from your clients, customers, patients, employees, managers, executives and stakeholders. These areas are the mobility of the business. Any where there is immobility it is important to mobilize. These six areas must be strengthening like exercise for the company, organization or business. Ergo Solutions has identified the E-Words for Administration and Management Stability.

xcellence

nergy

xercise

nterprising

xpanding

ducation

XCELLENCE

EXCELLENCE: *What is morally good, a theory or system of moral value; guiding philosophy; Skill or knowledge gained by doing something; direct observation of; practical knowledge skill or practice derived from direct observation.*

As a Physical Therapist I had to overcome burnout. It did not take long for me to feel the redundancy of "evaluate, treat, discharge." I quickly lost interest in shoulders, knees, backs and ankles. In a matter of 2 years I was ready for a change. It wasn't until after three years that I fully began to understand my profession more thoroughly. I started in the profession at 22 years old, fresh out of college. I had a lot of growing up and maturing before I understood myself as a professional. I had to study how to become more professional in excellence.

There are four keys to excellence in an educational model: developing cultural competence, professional identity information and engagement in the community practice and PT advocacy and reflection on experience. I adopted the mindset to embrace diversity and become more competent in treating all different types of people within all types of cultures. I studied many cultures and the topic of diversity. I wrote a diversity book, *White Man Black Man Chinese Man* that reflects multiculturalism in my workplace. I studied cultural competence, learning the definition as "acceptance and respect for difference, continuing self-assessment regarding culture, vigilance towards the dynamics of differences, ongoing expansion of cultural knowledge and resources, and adaptations to services."

I had to develop a professional identity through training students from universities throughout the United States that were in PT programs. I developed my technical skills and knowledge combined with my professional values which guided my clinical decision-making. I wanted to make a difference every day with my clients.

How important is Excellence to a company or organization? Business intelligence is meaningful data collected from "multiple sources" that analyzes "patterns, trends and relationships for strategic decision making" which can be manipulated and revolutionizes over time. – Baltzan.

These quality assurances will control and monitor quantitative tools and their efficiency:

EXCELLENCE

Day to day operations for Ergo Solutions consists of meeting staffing needs, customer services of daily care, productivity, revenue predicting, and expense control. The operations management has weekly, monthly and quarterly meetings to monitor data and make decisions for innovations, for adjusting staff, quality assurance, production, revenue and expense controls. Ergo Solutions uses predictive analytics to monitor these areas on a month-to-month basis. Ergo Solutions has invested in software to track and monitor for predictive analysis for evolution of the company. Ergo also uses Casamba, a health data information software system, for data input. The software enables the company to generate reports by grouping information into graphs and charts for user-friendly analyzing.

Predictive analytics uses statistics, modeling, machine learning and data mining that analyze current and historical facts to make predictions about future events. Ergo Solutions trained managers how to produce the available charts and reports that are made user-friendly in the Casamba System. Each manager must know data mining to track and monitor, as well as to report to the customers and the executive board. Each manager produces a weekly report of staff productivity, revenue generated, billed services, and time sheets for staff. Statistical analyzing is important for the managers to follow for overview of the Personnel and Compensation Committee (P&C) that review all reports.

EXCELLENCE-QUALITY ASSURANCE

According to Baltzan (2012), business intelligence is meaningful data collected from "multiple sources" that analyzes "patterns, trends and relationships for strategic decision making" which can be manipulated and revolutionized overtime. Ergo Solutions has developed a Quality Assurance plan for Information Systems throughout its store with new sources of methods, tools and techniques. Our new software will assist us with analyzing patterns and trends on how to staff, organize and operate efficiently and integrate compliance. Baltzan further stated that "successful" manager's compile, analyze, and comprehend massive amounts of data daily" in order to make "successful" business decisions. Our Chief Information Officer trains our managers to evaluate information systems relationships for strategic decision-making throughout project life cycles.

Training enables us to design, document and test programs to adequately comply with control and monitor metrics. The quality assurances control and monitor quantitative tools and its efficiency. Ergo Solutions maximizes the software to produce charts, forms and checklists that are user-friendly for quality function. We also ensure responsiveness to regulatory requirements. Ergo Solutions will be "more effective in decision making, more efficient in IT; freeing up resources for innovation and faster realization of value from IT investments".

TESTING

Ergo Solution's Quality Assurance (QA) team will organize, inform, execute, collect and coordinate automated testing efforts within the company. The store will use a web-based QA tool to centralize detailed records and files, that will be easy to use and test for managers within the QA team. Testing will assist leveraging in estimations and actualizations of project management within the store to predict outcomes of workload, revenue, productivity, costs, savings, sales, and more. Ergo Solutions utilizes real-time informational dashboards for controlling and monitoring outcomes in each department through integrated software information system. Companies should integrate business intelligence processes that interact with operational systems, they "can then react quickly to important events and identify the cause and effect relationships that are key to long term success." Tapscott concludes that companies that incorporate simple business intelligence processes can empower employees to make "real-time" quick effective decisions while remaining competitors in the ever-changing technology age."

Ergo Solutions will utilize web-based testing software for customer and suppliers to use and assess to freely customize integration of customer's needs. It will alert and notify managers of timelines and milestones for any bugs in the projects as well as overdue items and new issues.

TABLE 13 - EXCELLENCE EVALUATION TOOL

Complete table and totals to collect assessment.
Check the box of the "Yes" Column if the evaluation point applies to your organization;
Check the box of the "No" in the box if the evaluation point does not apply to your organization. Each "Yes" answer is worth 1.42 points, record the value in the - Point Value column. Add points in the Point Value column.

EXCELLENCE EVALUATION POINTS	YES (1.42 pts for each answer)	NO (0 pts for each answer)	POINT VALUE
Allocating QA time for training and Monitoring?			
Conducting Quality reviews of Application Systems and Data Processing?			
Initiating, Conducting and Reviewing QA systems?			
Validation of Systems reviews and testing in Reporting Results of QA audits?			
Improve Maintenance of Software systems?			
Developed Measures and Metrics of a QA manual?			
Track progress?			
TOTAL – *Degree Potential x10*			

ᴇNTHUSIAM

ᴇɴᴛʜᴜꜱɪᴀᴍ: *Strong excitement about something, a strong feeling of active interest in something that you like or enjoy.*[xxiii]

"To cultivate enthusiasm, create a business-focused, upscale, exclusive experience"- *Bob Spencer, Consultant Administrator*

As a senior therapist I had to learn to move out of my comfort zone into areas of greater responsibility. These are skills I needed to develop, "...vision, enthusiasm, and commitment to go the extra mile.

My passion for teaching was enabled by working with student physical therapists. I love to teach. I realize that when passion is incorporated into our work situation, it is both "life changing and energizing, along with creating the thrill of discovery and accomplishment."

As a senior therapist I gained enthusiasm for rehabilitation by exploring the possibility of combining my passions of leadership, teaching, and training to my work situation. I had to take on new challenges that pushed me beyond my normal comfort zone."

How important is Enthusiasm to a company or organization? Integrated communication within a centralized organization structure allows for effective span of control and functioning departments that promote the company. The marketing director should work closely with other department directors and manage the marketing department with a team focused on managing marketing operations.

Develop a social media campaign, inclusive to Linked-In, YouTube, Facebook, and Twitter. Social media can be a benefit to both customers and providers. Norton and Strauss share that "many health care organizations use Facebook and Twitter to: promote employee and community activities; communicate opportunities for better health; introduce new and advanced medical procedures; spotlight employee volunteer efforts; and keep employees and patients up-to-date on the impacts of weather-related events or emergencies.

Linked-in is a highly useful tool for recruiting in the community. YouTube can be helpful for management; providing educational and training that also drives traffic to corporate websites. Also, to evaluate effectiveness of social media using a macro model of communication.

Kotler and Keller suggest the "macro model of the communication process [that] first lists the two major parties in a communication—*sender* and *receiver*." Identify as the sender and be sensitive to the receiver in many ways. Study trends of marketing in sending messages through marketing channels that reach clients.

Kotler and Keller state there is a "major communication tool—*message* and *media*." The marketing team manages and controls messages to the community by: websites, brochures, materials, social media, face to face, advertisements, and public relations. Work to promote positivity in the community.

Kotler and Keller also suggest that "four elements represent major communication functions—*encoding*, *decoding*, *response*, and *feedback*." Decipher communication from clients and potential ones by understanding how they receive marketing; through the 8 modes of communication. How clients encode and decode marketing messages is highly important. Know "did they get it?" After marketing ask more questions about how information was received. Many different responses are common; understand the importance of paying close attention and listening to responses of clients and potential clients. Solicit feedback and learn from the experience.

Norton and Strauss shared that "many...organizations have policies on social media that instruct employees not to post anything at all about their job, their workday, or their patients. Training is the key to success — training, training, and more training." Be committed to training staff on the use of social media even where it is newly accepted.

Peter Drucker explains in *The Discipline of Innovation*, that innovation can be systemically managed through a process that includes internal and external oversight. In business it is important to consider that management for entrepreneurs consists of "talent, ingenuity and knowledge."

In 2013 Ergo hired a marketing strategist business development team leader to grow the other arm of Ergo Solutions called Ergo OccMed. With this position we gained a dedicated person to bring strategic planning, creativity and to gather knowledge from the therapists. This allowed us to record organic knowledge and ensure our services are consistent, repeatable and held to a high standard; then shared that perspective with our customer, clients and patients as applicable; this also created for our organization a way to establish and share our selves as subject matter experts. We used what we gained to highlight our presence to various organizations. This also grew our business naturally and expanded our opportunity to present externally.

Creativity, innovation, ingenuity: Creativity must be integrated into a strategy - Robert Sutton's three videos on the importance of implementation and how critical is it. Basically, if you are not using the knowledge gained through the processes to create, innovate and invent - then you are wasting the corporate time and resources. Creative implementation will lead to innovation; developed by new ideas and new ingenuity. Companies are encouraged to continue to develop marketing ideas. Import new strategy and new knowledge but not to recreate the wheel.

The positioning strategy is "the activities undertaken by the marketer to communicate the features and the benefits of the product and the image of the brand to the actual and potential customers." Ergo Solutions has a team of marketers, which is every owner, executive and staff member to promote and market Ergo Solutions in a positive way. The branding of Ergo Solutions lies within the people of Ergo Solutions. We realize the importance of word-of- mouth marketing for recruiting and marketing for therapists.

Ergo Solutions must market to new opportunities in the hospital and nursing home industry to provide rehab services. We market at conferences, direct face to face and trainings. The customer segments vary in different types of hospitals and nursing homes. Some hospitals are acute care, long-term acute care or rehabilitation hospitals. Nursing homes vary by short-term or long-term care with different needs of care like orthopedics, neurologic, debilitative or a hybrid of all. Ergo Solutions market to the various segments by our strengths and abilities.

The positioning strategies are divided into three classifications as follows: "1. Target customers, 2. Target competitors, and 3. Competitive advantages." Ergo Solutions uses positioning strategies to remain competitive in the rehab industry. We target our customers in segments that work for Ergo Solutions. We make impact with interning therapists through relationships built on education. We position our company in mid-Atlantic, Northeastern and Southeastern Universities through educational internships. Target customers are "customers with the highest attractiveness for the organization who bring the highest gains." Ergo Solutions target customers in this highly competitive industry, and it's important to play to our strengths.

For Ergo Solutions to remain competitive in the rehab industry we have "priority among equal level service, having value-added in compared to service price, reliability, attractiveness, country of origin, innovation, brand, and service social class." These are the eight characteristics that all companies in our industry must do to survive.

Ergo Solutions uses more of a "pull strategy which uses advertising, promotion, and other forms of communication to persuade consumers to demand the product from intermediaries." Our "vertical marketing systems" is inclusive to a corporate marketing director, that leads an executive marketing committee that assist in advertising and promoting Ergo Solutions' in the rehab community. Our pull strategy is to persuade new business through intermediate channels to reach new customers and markets.

We have identified those other vendors that interrelate with and expose us to more possible customers. We have marketing channels with orthoptists, prosthetists, wheelchair and durable medical equipment companies that open channels for new customers. Physicians that refer clients to rehab serve as another channel for us to provide our service product to the customer.

Ergo Solutions builds with like-minded organizations to serve relative function towards our sustainability by their ability to "gather information, develop and disseminate persuasive communications, reach agreements on price and terms, and assume some risks."

Ergo Solutions has used on-line marketing approaches to reach new channels to gain new customers. We market to build new partnerships and develop leads to ensure future business.

TABLE 14 -
ENTHUSIASM EVALUATION TOOL

Complete table and totals to collect assessment.
Check the box of the "Yes" Column if the evaluation point applies to your organization;
Check the box of the "No" in the box if the evaluation point does not apply to your
organization. Each "Yes" answer is worth 1.0 points, record the value in the - Point
Value column. Add points in the Point Value column.

ENTHUSIASM EVALUATION POINTS	YES (1.0 pts for each answer)	NO (0 pts for each answer)	POINT VALUE
Choosing to be excited about what needs to be done?			
Contagious Incentive and Collective By-In?			
Morale – Organizational Climate?			
Creating pleasant experiences?			
Interaction?			
Rewards Delivery and Positive results?			
Project Sincerity?			
Reflecting Positive?			
Attentive?			
Selection Criteria for success?			
TOTAL – *Degree Potential x10*			

ENERGY

ENERGY: *The physical or mental strength that allows you to do something. A fundamental entity of nature that is transferred between parts of a system in the production of physical change within the system and usually regarded as the capacity for doing work.*

"The Ergo Way is full of passion, energy, (and) excitement ...a sense of being genuine ...and related to humor. Another word...is elation, because it (the Ergo Way) is contagious"- *Sue Hargreaves, LLDH Home*

Being a manager of outpatient rehab requires a lot of energy for the high volume of patients. I learned to manage time, caseload, documentation, billing and provide quality care. I remember having days of seeing 18-20 patients per day. Energy is spent greatly in a work day. I would go home spent after a full day of patient care. I had to learn to maintain energy and keep it up for every patient that I would see.

As a manager I understand the demand of productivity and need to meet required demands of work of staff. The therapists that I led and managed would share how high demands of work would exhaust them so I had to manage expenditure rate of PT tasks. I had to learn about working with an energy expenditure rate. Fatigue factor is important to consider in doing health care like nursing, and therapy. The maximum energy expenditure rate of the tasks will decrease work productivity performance due to the onset of physical fatigue.

How important is Energy to a company or organization? Coach John Wooden says that at the top of his success pyramid is competitive greatness. To be a great competitor in their industry, energy is required. The physical and mental strength in effective training counters weak leadership and ineffective succession. This will place a company in a noncompetitive position in the marketplace.

Positive energy in business allows continuous investment in our employees from within for leadership positions and elevation. It also suggests that there is a high possibility of hiring from within and developing "fast track training" to senior positions. Feeding the business encourages the staff to work, develop their skills and be creative to innovate new ways of service and learn the best practices. It is not enough to encourage staff; Jodi Chavez shares that succession planning is also highly necessary. She addresses the relationships that exist between the successor and the emerging leader. The process of transferring leadership to an emerging talent can be intimidating and - can sometimes be faulty. She shares the benchmarks for looking for a successor in business. In the John Wooden model, there are energetic key characteristics that a leader must look for in those to whom they will pass the torch. Emerging leaders ought to be "visionaries with heart, passion, energy, courage and integrity." John Wooden also talks about the cornerstone of his model is enthusiasm. Chavez speaks similarly to Wooden about a passionate emergent leader. Chavez says an emergent leader should be an "open minded peer who listens and learns from others." On the Wooden model, energy is "cooperation: the ability to work with others." Chavez shares three factors of succession planning:

1. "Identifying successors and emerging leaders
2. Developing and engaging employees for leadership.
3. Retaining proven performers."

In identifying successors, Ergo Solutions has an executive body of 12 executives. Training is done monthly with this group to keep the team growing and developing. The loss of a key executive can and is costly for a company to replace. This team identifies emerging leaders from within.

In developing and engaging employees for leadership, Ergo Solutions adopts the teaching of energetic leadership and succession planning. The engagements to employees are important to knowing who may be the next generation of future executives. Chavez suggests looking for experience from emerging leaders in "volunteerism and community service, nonprofit board experience, and participation in industry and professional groups." The Wooden model expresses the need for energetic "industriousness," with corporate members who have developed their skills and share an intensity to continue growing their talents.

Retention programs must to consider the energy of "time, expense, and missed opportunity incurred with the recruitment, hiring and training of new talent." When succession occurs within an organization, there should be less time needed for growth and development for the emerging leaders. To cut down recruiting, it's good to have a person already prepared for the future opportunity from within.

TABLE 15 -
ENERGY EVALUATION TOOL

Complete table and totals to collect assessment.
Check the box of the "Yes" Column if the evaluation point applies to your organization; Check the box of the "No" in the box if the evaluation point does not apply to your organization. Each "Yes" answer is worth 1.0 points, record the value in the - Point Value column. Add points in the Point Value column.

ENERGY EVALUATION POINTS	YES (1.0 pts for each answer)	NO (0 pts for each answer)	POINT VALUE
Project Completion?			
Initiative to complete projects?			
Due Diligence – Fatal Flaw analysis?			
Validation of Concept?			
Work Concept optimization?			
Secure binding agreement?			
Development?			
Constructive assessments and structured services?			
Managing Operation and ROI?			
Sustainability?			
Ability to Manage Work?			
TOTAL – *Degree Potential x10*			

# ENTERPRISING

ENTERPRISING: *Marked by an independent energetic spirit and by readiness to act.*

"The Ergo Way is not (being) afraid to explore creative and expanding concept, discovering new ideas of service and taking to the marketplace-thinking outside the box"- *Henry Vaughn, CFO of Capitol Hill Hospital*

"Bold, undertaking to make profits through monopoly with business to obtain"- *George Brownlee, Principle of Ergo Solutions*

As a Director for another company, I have learned enterprising through information management, networking and planning and strategizing. My first attempt at enterprising was at my corporate company's expense. I had to deliver executive officer-level management businesses engagement in a strategic planning process. As a director, I studied leading management theorists who consider the environment to be the major determinant of organizational structure, internal processes, and managerial decision making.

Alongside my study, I had a mentor who shared with me that I should focus to develop my skills and qualities with customers, competitors, regulatory issues, socio-cultural-political, economic, and technological servicing. I also learned from other directors, how to be tactical, making sure of their employees, who are engaged in a specialized practice, all while growing high net incomes for their business.

I was working for other companies as if they were my own. I had developed skills and abilities to the degree of proficiency in technological and marketing environments to make concrete business decisions for someone else.

How important is Enterprising to a company or organization? A business plan takes all the energy and motivation in the organization and channels it all in to a well thought-out detailed plan. When done well, it covers each aspect of an enterprising organization, ensuring a balanced effort is directed towards these areas, and it focuses on the key areas required to reach goals. Just the act of writing a business plan, even if it is never opened again, will help clarify where the energy is in an enterprising organization.

STRATEGIC PLANNING

The first step to enterprising is strategic planning. Strategic planning is a chance to look outside of 'the way things are done' and take a fresh look at problems with new information and learning. For example, the needs of an area would be very different before an organization existed. Now that there is an organization, new and deeper needs may present themselves. There is a need to step back and look with a broadened perspective at the needs of possible clients and customers.

Strategic planning is a chance to involve stakeholders. This includes family, staff and board members, funders – anyone who has a stake in the enterprising organization. Use them as a sounding board, ask them what you do well and where you are deficient. Ask them what is important to them. Study their environment and pay interest to the changes. Make personal observations by assessing how well the needs of local families are met. Given these observations, are the needs of the stakeholders met? What should you do to make sure of this? From here, a guiding compass – the vision and mission – is developed. The compass should create energy around a common vision of the future and how you are going to get there. This is your opportunity to dream; to picture the world as you would like to see it.

Next, you need to develop the road map: strategic priorities and definite goals. What do you need to do well to support your mission and achieve your vision? How will you know when you have been successful? Set targets using balanced-strategic priorities to ensure organization growth. For example, Ergo Solutions provides enterprising services in nursing homes and hospitals. We contract with facilities and establish a term for contract pricing of services. Ergo Solutions has three primary ways to negotiate pricing to win an awarded contract with a nursing home. The provider facility produces the bills for reimbursement from the insurance, either Medicare A, B, or Medicare. The reimbursed payment is then negotiated with Ergo Solutions for its portion of providing the services that enable the facility to bill. Ergo Solutions uses going-rate pricing, value pricing and target return pricing.

TABLE 16 - ENTERPRISING EVALUATION TOOL

Complete table and totals to collect assessment.
Check the box of the "Yes" Column if the evaluation point applies to your organization;
Check the box of the "No" in the box if the evaluation point does not apply to your
organization. Each "Yes" answer is worth 1.25 points, record the value in the - Point
Value column. Add points in the Point Value column.

ENTERPRISING EVALUATION POINTS	YES (1.25 pts for each answer)	NO (0 pts for each answer)	POINT VALUE
Integrated logistics system?			
Materials management?			
Material flow systems?			
Physical distribution?			
Information technology?			
Business intelligence?			
Forecasting?			
Scheduling?			
TOTAL – Degree Potential x10			

XPANDING

EXPANDING: *Increasing in size, range or amount or make bigger.*

"Exponential growth while exceeding goals" - *Courtland Wyatt, Principal of Ergo Solutions and Ergo OccMed*

I was given a chief officer role. It required me to grow personally because previously I had been a clinician with my primary focus being patient care. To take on my role, I increased my ability to diversify by creating relationships that fostered and sustained my business focus. I learned the practice of growth for expansion. The organizational structure of the company needed to expand. Networking, strategic planning, and information management were key.

How important is Expanding to a company or organization? Marketing allows promotion, shared experience, advertising, and socializing with others about what is being offered for sale. Marketing is not just advertising, it is exposure market and the diversity of the market – channel systems are a means of expansion. Kotler and Keller suggest "a marketing channel system is the particular set of interdependent organizations involved in the process of making a product or service available for use or consumption." Social networks are powerful effective marketing tools that can expand, define, and identify the market. These tools make sure a company can measure the value of a market. A company should know the value of their product to the market they are selling to and the value of the market they are selling in.

Kotler and Keller suggest "a marketing information system consists of people, equipment, and procedures to gather, sort, analyze, evaluate, and distribute needed, timely, and accurate information to marketing decision makers." A business owner should implement a strategic plan and set a balance scorecard with marketing metrics. Industry specialist, Lusch suggests that CMOs, CFOs and CEOs set specific goals for each metric. Still, as corporate goals are set, expanding and measuring will communicate and signal the organization, that new products and market development are critical to future success.

Lusch also offers marketing structure goals - "An expanding organization must obtain competitive advantage. This is where a company can perform a service that the competitor cannot match." Set metrics to lead marketing by measuring "percent of sales from products introduced in the last three years; percent growth expansion projected over the next three years in size of target market, percent of sales over the last three years from trending market data; percent of time CEO spends on strategic marketing, percent of senior marketing executives whose work is focused to market analysis; percent of unsuccessful sales calls, unsuccessful new products, unsuccessful new advertising programs, or unsuccessful marketing initiatives, price-earnings relative to the top competitor, share of total market valuation today vs. five years ago, break-even sales as a percent of current sales and percent of customers over the last year who had an unsatisfactory service experience." It is critical to corporate capability and capacity that actions are made to compare and study the collective.

Management should come boldly to marketing even after mild to moderate expansion successes. Develop credentialed relationships to build corporate resume, profile, and reputation worthy of recommendations. New expanding opportunities will rise, and the organization will be able to develop other and more diversified accounts and contracts - particularly, staffing contracts. Seek opportunities to put people to work.

For example, through marketing in the Washington, DC area, Ergo Solutions began staff augmentation and project expansion based staffing assignments. We gained contract assignments in 2004-2007 with reputable organizations such as, Providence Hospital, Carroll Manor Nursing Home, Hadley Memorial Hospital, Greater Southeast Hospital, Howard University and others.

The best story that I remember was a cold-contact gorilla market attempt at Hadley Memorial Hospital. The marketing began when we walked in to a facility that we identified - through market study - as 'in need of therapist.' We entered the Hadley Memorial Hospital and asked to speak with an administrator. We were introduced to the administrator, who granted us an opportunity to offer our corporate services to her team and herself: The director of nursing, a CPA, and other clinical specialists.

We set our goal to providing management of the physical therapy department and we began doing so in 2007. We grew with staffing contracts, market share and leadership development; however, study proved we needed to make sure we could afford to grow:

- Expanding is sustained growth.
- Enterprising is marketing to beat of the threat of growing too fast without enough capital.

TABLE 17 - EXPANSION EVALUATION TOOL

Complete table and totals to collect assessment.
Check the box of the "Yes" Column if the evaluation point applies to your organization;
Check the box of the "No" in the box if the evaluation point does not apply to your
organization. Each "Yes" answer is worth 1.0 points, record the value in the - Point
Value column. Add points in the Point Value column.

EXPANSION EVALUATION POINTS	YES (1.0 pts for each answer)	NO (0 pts for each answer)	POINT VALUE
Risk Assessment for Growth?			
Plan for Growth?			
Human Resources to match expansion needs?			
Management readiness			
Operating Cost Assessment?			
Equipment?			
Proximity?			
Quality of Labor?			
Clustering – Leverage workforce?			
Quality of Life?			
Cost and risk of Business disruption?			
Choose to Expand?			
TOTAL – *Degree Potential x10*			

# DUCATION

EDUCATION: *The knowledge, skill and understanding that you get from attending school, college or university.*

"Educated employees are the best resources. Educated employees pay back tenfold. It is a return on investment (ROI). We hire for careers, not for jobs." - *Gail Jernigan, Administrator, Transitions Nursing home, DCHCA 2015 Administrator of the Year*

"Education is a powerful weapon ... An educated man can't learn enough. It is said 'educate a woman and educate a generation." - *Dr. Lynda Woodruff, Educator, Professor Alabama State University, Georgia State University*

How *important is Education to a company or organization?* When managers act on better logic and evidence, their companies outdo competition. That is why we've spent our entire research careers, especially the last five years, working to develop and discover the best evidence on how companies ought to be managed and teaching managers the right mindset and methods for practicing evidence-based management. As with medicine, management is and will likely always be a craft that can be learned only through practice and experience. Yet we believe that managers (like doctors) can practice their craft more effectively if they are routinely guided by the best logic and evidence—and if they relentlessly seek new knowledge and insight, from both inside and outside their companies, to keep updating their assumptions, knowledge, and skills. We aren't there yet, but we are getting closer. The managers and companies that come closest already enjoy a pronounced competitive advantage:

- Expenses
- Exploration (research)
- Expectations

"Inputs like marketing research, and external data to establish processing in our marketing information system. The model we establish is determined by a decision support system (DSS) that monitors information from specialist to direct marketing outcomes."[xxiv]

Education is critical to growth. Continued education is necessary for staying up-to-date in the profession. How do you get ahead? Education can be formal or informal;

however it's important to stay ahead of competition with cutting-edge approaches. We are able to market ourselves with degrees, certifications, advanced education and trainings.

Ergo Solutions is in the rehab industry along with our competitors. Each company in this industry faces the same critical concerns for marketing for survival. The issue with focusing on the core market as the best strategy for a company comes in when the company has competitors that do the same things or provide the same service. To continue to remain profitable in a competitive environment, "an organization must obtain the competitive advantage. This is where a company can perform a service that the competitor cannot match."

Learning new skills and specializations through education enables a company to grow. Ergo Solutions has market segments in differing areas and segments within each area. For example, each company markets to recruit therapists to provide services. Ergo Solutions has marketed to segments of therapists. We market to new graduates from area accredited colleges with programs at Howard University, George Washington University, Marymount University, Maryland Eastern Shore and others. We market to therapists that practice in the area and people who may be interested in working in the Nation's capital.

Education gives us tangible and intangible power. Intellectual capacity can be quite intangible but manifests in positive outcomes. Ergo Solutions provides specialized consultant services in each model to assist the hospitals and nursing homes to be as effective in each area. Ergo Solutions realized that customer training is needed to "operate the department properly and efficiently."

TABLE 18 -
DUCATION EVALUATION TOOL

Complete table and totals to collect assessment.
Check the box of the "Yes" Column if the evaluation point applies to your organization;
Check the box of the "No" in the box if the evaluation point does not apply to your organization. Each "Yes" answer is worth 0.9 points, record the value in the - Point Value column. Add points in the Point Value column.

EDUCATION EVALUATION POINTS	YES (0.9 pts for each answer)	NO (0 pts for each answer)	POINT VALUE
Provide resources for Continuing Education?			
In-service Training?			
Technology – Distance Based learning?			
Relationships with area Universities and Education Experts?			
Do you Foster Education opportunities?			
Reward scholarship?			
Procedure, process and policy that guides education opportunity?			
Education Leadership – Executive implementation of skilled gained?			
Initiative to foster knowledge sharing and organizational learning?			
Future leadership training?			
Peer learning?			
TOTAL – Degree Potential x10			

REFERENCES

i   Highly selective public high school in Philadelphia, PA – Student are drawn from all parts of the city.

ii   FAMU, Tallahasse, FL – Home of the Rattlers

iii   Meaning measurable - capable of being measured or expressed in numerical terms – Encarta Dictionary

iv   Meaning a relationship to or based on the quality or character of something, often as opposed to its size or quantity – Encarta Dictionary

v   Washington DC metropolitan statistical area – US Census defined

vi   Merriam-Webster

vii   Kaplan 1997

viii   Merriam-Webster

ix   Merriam-Webster

x   Norton, 2010, www.irr-hungary.hu

xi   Kaplan Strategy & Leadership 1996

xii   Inamdar, Kaplan, Journal of Healthcare Management, 2002

xiii   Profit & Loss

xiv   Kaplan 1997

xv   www.investopedia.com

xvi   A factorial is a total achieved by multiplying all numbers up to a particular number, for our purposes, it is an equation built to show the product of a standard evaluated by all the perspectives below it. "In business - involving or characteristic of a commercial factor or the work of such a factor." –Encarta dictionary.

xvii   Brueller and Carmeli

xviii   Merriam-Webster

xix   Merriam-Webster

xx   Goleman, D, "The Emotional Intelligence of Leaders" Leader to Leaders p.20-26

xxi   From Investopedia.com -Definition of 'Brand Equity': The value premium that a company realizes from a product with a recognizable name as compared to its generic equivalent. Companies can create brand equity for their products by making them memorable, easily recognizable and superior in quality and reliability. Mass marketing campaigns can also help to create brand equity. If consumers are willing to pay more for a generic product than for a branded one, however, the brand is said to have negative brand equity. This might happen if a company had a major product recall or caused a widely publicized environmental disaster.

xxii   From Wisegeek.net- Organizational career development looks closely at how employees at various levels perceive and interact with their work environments. The goal of such an assessment is to develop new strategies to encourage employee communication, satisfaction and retention, as well as to improve a company's bottom line. Organizational career development is a valuable long-term planning tool used to create better and more productive work environments.

xxiii   "Enthusiasm." Merriam-Webster.com. Accessed March 26, 2016. http://www.merriam-webster.com/dictionary/enthusiasm

xxiv   Kotler and Keller, 2010, p. 151

ABOUT THE AUTHOR

JASON **HENDERSON** is the Chief Executive Officer of Ergo Solutions LLC and Executive Director of Ergo Resolutions Inc., companies based in Washington, D.C.

His clients include the American Academy of Physical Therapy, District of Columbia Health Care Association, Maryland Health Care Association, and the D.C. Board of Nursing, among many others. As a Doctor of Physical Therapy, he teaches, consults and presents to many organizations across the United States.

Since 2001, Jason has served as a dynamic public speaker. His focus includes issues related to leadership, consumer service, recruiting and retention, training and development, marketing and branding, and a host of other topics critical to business.

Jason also contributes to various publications and other media as a health care disparities expert. As a cum laude graduate of Florida A&M University, he earned a Bachelor of Science degree in Physical Therapy; he earned a Doctorate in Physical Therapy from Alabama State University, and completed a Master of Business Administration from University Of Maryland University College.

Dr. Henderson, DPT, MBA is a Philadelphia Native.

CONTACT THE AUTHOR

Dr. Jason Henderson, DPT
jhenderson@ergo180.com
(240) 417-2502

When you write, please include your testimonial
or tell me how this book helped you in any way.
I'd love to hear from you.

To Purchase Additional Books:

www.OptimisticDiversity.com
www.amazon.com
Also available on Kindle
www.anointedpressgraphics.com

For Bulk Orders over 25 books, call
Anointed Press Publishers, (301) 782-2285

INGRAM DISTRIBUTION